Community Wisdom 2

Tips, Ideas, and Thoughts for Community Success

by

Maury Forman
Jim Mooney

Introduction by

Martha Choe
Director
Washington State Department of Community, Trade and Economic Development

Cartoons by

Chris Britt

KENDALL/HUNT PUBLISHING COMPANY
4050 Westmark Drive   Dubuque, Iowa 52002

Introduction

It takes wisdom, focus, and hard work to lay the foundation for a strong and vital economy—one job at a time.

Have you ever wondered if your children can have better jobs than we do? Will they have to move 100, 1,000, or even 5,000 miles away to a different city, state, country, or continent to get a good job that they love? Or will they be able to find a prosperous enough future to raise their own families in the same communities that you did?

Community Wisdom 2 speaks to how communities create the kinds of jobs and prosperity we want for our future generations. It speaks to how we as economic development professionals use our creativity, our partners, and our many assets to craft a bona fide strategy for strong and sustainable economic growth. It speaks to the lessons learned through real success stories and the men and women who work so hard to actually create the jobs that our sons and daughters will want one day.

As the nation and the state continue to experience slow economic recovery, we're all asking those questions—and we're grateful to have resources like *Community Wisdom 2* as we work to strengthen our communities and develop positive answers.

Martha Choe
Director
Washington State Department of Community, Trade and Economic Development

Acknowledgments

*A true friend is one who overlooks your failures
and tolerates your success.*

— DOUG LARSON

We have been fortunate to have a number of people who have contributed to *Community Wisdom 2*. Without these people, the sayings, ideas, and thoughts in this book would still be rolling around in our heads.

♦ Martha Choe, Director of the Washington State Department of Community, Trade and Economic Development, who has created an environment that allows staff to take the ball and run with it, even if it doesn't always score.

♦ Robin Pollard, Assistant Director for the Washington State Department of Community, Trade and Economic Development, who has mentored her staff to have fun and enjoy the work they do.

♦ Cathy Swirbul, CHS Communications, for doing an excellent job in editing an array of thoughts that came to our minds, and Evelyn Roehl of Flying Fingers, who was responsible for the layout that makes the book so readable.

♦ Willie Bodger, Technical Support with the Washington State Department of Community Trade and Economic Development, who has helped save this publication numerous times from landing in cyberspace.

♦ Don Iannone, Mark James, Roger Brooks, and Christine Lemon, who are considered three of the best and brightest consultants working in the field of economic development today. They still found time to contribute a number of sections for the book.

♦ And finally, Chris Britt, cartoonist extraordinaire, whose work makes practitioners realize that this profession can be fun as well as satisfying.

We consider these people not only to be our colleagues but also our friends, and we greatly appreciate their work and their ability to bask in our success.

Attribution

The Internet is a wonderful tool to look for quotes and sayings. Unfortunately, it is not as good when it comes to finding the original source. Every effort was made to find the authors of the sayings and quotes in this book. Since personal credit was not always available, the authors apologize to those people whom we have omitted and thank them for their wit and wisdom.

About the Authors

Maury Forman is the Director of Education and Training for the Washington State Department of Community Trade and Economic Development. He was the winner of the American Economic Development Council's Preston Award for outstanding contributions in educational advancement, the ROI Research Institute Award for Innovation in Adult Education, and the U.S. Small Business Administration's Vision 2000 Award for program excellence. He was also honored by the Inland Northwest Partners into their Hall of Fame for his support of economic development education in the region. He is the author of numerous books, including *The Washington Entrepreneurs Guide, How To Create Jobs Now and Beyond 2000, Learning to Lead, Race to Recruit, Community Wisdom,* and *The 25 Immutable Rules of Successful Tourism.*

Jim Mooney is president of DeSCo, an economic development consulting agency providing organizational and technical services to people and organizations. Jim has been a practicing economic developer for 20 years with a career that has provided the opportunity to serve customers in both the private and public sector. While a practitioner, Jim developed an expertise for organizational start-ups and turn-arounds giving him first hand experience at making an economic development organization a successful venture. He also specialized in business attraction efforts that provided him the opportunity to travel and interact with customers in the American, European and Asian economic sectors. He has published three books on economic development: *Doing the Deal—a Developer's Guide to Effective Incentive Utilization, The Race to Recruit,* and *Learning to Lead,* as well as numerous articles that have appeared in trade and professional publications. He also instructs deal-negotiating classes at five universities throughout the United States.

Contributors

Roger Brooks
Destination Development
Olympia, Washington

Russ Campbell
Washington State Department of Community Trade
and Economic Development
Seattle, Washington

Gayla Harris
Healthyself
Austin, Texas

Don Iannone
Donald T. Iannone & Associates
Mayfield Village, Ohio

Mark James
ED Solutions, Inc.
Dublin, Ohio

Christine Lemon
Chelsea House International, Inc.
Westerville, Ohio

Robin Roberts
Governor's Community Solutions and
Economic Revitalization Office
Portland, Oregon

Tim Stearns
Washington State Department of Community Trade
and Economic Development
Seattle, Washington

Community

Wisdom 2

I have a game plan.
I just don't have a game.

When you ask CEOs what they attribute their success to, they'll tell you about business plans, strategic plans, and game plans. To them, the word "plan" is not a four-letter word. Their experience shows that planning pays off. While planning alone does not result in the action needed to get the job done, trying to act without a well-conceived plan results in wasted time.

Economic development plans should be written as business plans. After all, economic development *is* a business, not a hobby or a part-time job. A step-by-step planning process enables a community to agree on how to achieve an economic development vision. That vision is like a compass, a guide for where you want to go. It is not a placebo. It will help the community to understand its economy, to focus on the right things, and to inform and coordinate the public and private resources required to accomplish their stated goals and objectives.

While some communities create a plan and let it gather dust, others become so rigid that they are unable to achieve results because they leave no room for adapting to a changing environment. In prehistoric times, we are told, sharks and dinosaurs lived in the same periods. The dinosaur, full of bones and not very flexible, did not adjust and adapt. The shark, which does not have a bone in its body, only cartilage, made it to modern times. Economic development plans should be like sharks, not dinosaurs. Everybody knows that sharks have game.

*I am not a vegetarian
because I love animals.
I am a vegetarian because
I hate plants.*

— A. WHITNEY BROWN

What motivates the movers and shakers in our communities? They often do things for reasons other than those that we fully understand or what is reported in the media. Successful economic developers learn who's who in the community and understand what compels them to act.

One of the first things economic developers need to do is identify the twelve most influential people in town. Often, they are not the ones sitting on the dais at the Council meetings. They are merely the "voice" of the power base in the community.

Once the top twelve are identified, the economic developers should create a résumé on each person. This isn't your normal résumé; it's one that identifies their links in the community, their history, and their major interests and/or hot buttons. These résumés will reveal a picture of the power network.

Once the power base is identified and understood, economic developers will have planted themselves securely in the community. This foundation will allow them to dine with the leadership while they devour the deals that offer their community the nutrition for a new tomorrow.

Horse sense is the thing a horse has that keeps it from betting on people.

— W. C. FIELDS

As an economic development practitioner, the stakeholders in your community are betting on you. Businesses expect practical services and help acquiring resources that make them more competitive and profitable. Government agencies want help in expanding their tax base to provide much needed community services. Workers expect higher-quality job and career opportunities that create more prosperity for them and their families. Schools, colleges, and universities need help in creating and finding the best jobs for their graduates. Everyone wants to raise the general quality of life in the community.

Practitioners need to understand who their stakeholders are and what they expect from the economic development organization. The organization, like the entities they serve, must create more value for their stakeholders if they are to survive and thrive in the future.

Remember that value, like beauty, exists in the eyes of the beholder. If you can demonstrate how your organization uses the financial and other support it receives to benefit your stakeholders and the community at large, they will be more convinced that it is valuable. Don't assume people understand the value you create for them. Make sure your next annual report speaks clearly about how stakeholders' expectations are being met. Then the community will start betting on your success.

If you want a kitten,
start out asking for a horse.

We learned the lesson at a very early age: if you ask for more than you need, you are more than likely to get what you want. It worked for us when we were young, and it works for us when we get older. Yet too many people forget that an economic development program will cost a community something, and they need to raise the money. A poorly funded program is the same as not having an economic development program at all.

To raise money for your economic development efforts, consider the following: One, maintain a membership-based organization for which dues are collected. Some organizations create a dues structure so that membership can benefit people, businesses, and organizations from throughout the community rather than just being for those that can pay. Economic development is for the entire community, and everyone should be able to provide input, regardless of whether or not they are members.

Two, obtain grants from city, state, and federal governments; private foundations; and private corporations. Find grants whose goals are closely associated with the community's goals. Targeting your proposal to the right funding agency will save time and money and increase the chances of success. (This may not be the right place to ask for a horse when you only need a kitten. Chances are that you won't get anything.)

Three, create an event. Partner with other groups to raise money that will support all of your activities. Successful events may not only get you a horse, but possibly an elephant as well.

Opportunity is missed by most people because it is dressed in overalls and looks like work.

— THOMAS EDISON

When opportunity knocks, some people won't answer the door. They are afraid that they must work hard to benefit from opportunity. In economic development, communities must do more than open the door to opportunity, because it may be a long time before the door opens again.

In Washington state, Governor Gary Locke has opened the door and welcomed the opportunity culture, saying it "promotes equality while celebrating diversity." This culture supports a first-class educational system for all ethnic groups, both genders, rural and urban, and rich and poor individuals. Governor Locke believes education is the great equalizer that will lead to a prosperous economy.

A world-class, all-inclusive education system will supply a first-rate, diverse workforce that will allow communities to keep and grow existing businesses. This education will attract industries of the future, such as software development. Communities need both traditional and new industries to create economic agility and a sustainable edge in the changing global economy.

An opportunity culture is, according to Locke, one in which "world-class education, knowledge-based economic competitiveness, priority-focused government, and engaged citizens work together toward shared and sustainable values." Communities should not shy away from what they see when they open the door. It will be hard work, but if you welcome opportunity into your home and feed it, it will stay and help you prosper.

Time is a circus, always packing up and moving away.

— Ben Hecht

If you are not taking care of your existing businesses, it will only be a matter of time before they decide to relocate to another community. Business retention programs are the backbone of any economic development strategy. A business retention program will create a healthy local economy and a strong business climate.

Often, the best chance of creating new jobs for a community comes from existing businesses. Businesses that stay competitive are more likely to remain in the community and possibly expand. Research indicates that they will be responsible for creating between 60 and 90 percent of all future jobs. That's why community leaders should keep track of who is hiring, who is cutting back, who is looking for more space, and what is standing in the way of growth.

Existing businesses will become more competitive if practitioners take the time and effort to evaluate and address some of their key needs and concerns. By working with local firms to address common business concerns, the community helps to ensure a healthier future for itself. Business retention also establishes an economic development plan for the community and a broad-based community coalition to sustain long-term economic development efforts.

Existing businesses should be treated as though they are the "greatest show on earth." Only then will they be encouraged to stay where they are rather than move from town to town.

Time is nature's way of keeping everything from happening all at once.

— WOODY ALLEN

When an economic developer takes a new position in a community, he or she can become overwhelmed by the scope of work that must be accomplished. The developer feels the need to get everything started at once, even though he or she knows that isn't reasonable or possible. Planning the sequence of tasks is essential for both professional success and personal sanity.

First, the developer should establish an economic baseline. Then, he or she can assess the community's strengths and weaknesses. The developer can set priorities for achievement through strategic planning sessions, then implement a step-by-step plan.

Once this process is put into place, a continual cycle of "plan–do–check–act" is important. The developer must analyze the situation, create a plan of action, and then check the results after the plan is implemented. Analyzing the results will help the developer create the next steps in the plan. This process takes time, but achieves the desired results.

Every journey of 1,000 miles begins with a single step, according to a Chinese proverb. Nature's requirement of taking things one step at a time helps to make community changes more successful by phasing in change sequentially rather than all at once. When this happens, the community will support and appreciate the changes more than if change is thrust upon them.

Culture is roughly anything we do that monkeys don't.

— LORD RAGLIN

For years, scientists and mathematicians believed that, given an infinite number of monkeys and an infinite number of typewriters, the monkeys would eventually write a great play or beautiful poems. Great works of culture would be produced. This theory was finally tested when students at Plymouth University in England put six monkeys in a room with computers. The results indicate that neither the comprehensive works of William Shakespeare nor the poetic genius of Henry Longfellow were threatened. Not only did the monkeys fail to type a single word, but they also ended up destroying the equipment.

Creating a cultural environment in a community is catching on as an effective economic development strategy. Not only do the arts create jobs, studies have shown America's nonprofit arts industry generates $134 billion in economic activity every year, including $24.4 billion in federal, state, and local tax revenues. In addition, attendance at arts events generates nearly $81 billion in related spending at hotels, restaurants, parking garages, and other establishments. This strategy has proven to be an economic stimulus in large and small communities, as art centers have sprung up in Port Townsend, Washington; Ketchum, Idaho; and Carmel, California. These communities began with local support of the arts and transformed themselves into national attractions.

Cultural activities are a significant industry in the United States. Communities that include the arts in their economic development strategy find it more productive than a roomful of monkeys with computers.

Give a man a fish and you feed him for a day, teach him to use the Net and he won't bother you for weeks.

There are a lot of economic development web sites out there. The more technology gets used in these sites, the higher the bar for what prospects expect. Prospects spend a great deal of time on the Internet and have become very dependent and proficient in looking at sites and making decisions from the comfort of their homes or offices. In order to keep them on your web site, practitioners must make sure that certain features are included.

First, you need to have plenty of valuable data. The more data, the better. In the initial search, if verifiable information is not on the site, your community could be quickly eliminated.

Second, make sure that the data is available in download-able formats. Provide options of both PDF (Portable Document) formats and Microsoft Excel tables. This allows the user to use the data to analyze and compare locations.

Third, the front page of your web site should always have geographic references, with a map of the entire region. Remember, prospects do not look at communities; they look at regions.

Finally, include contact information on every page: name of an individual, e-mail address, and phone and fax numbers.

The best economic development sites are data-rich, easy to navigate, clean-looking treasure troves of content that will entertain a prospect for weeks. By the time prospects are done looking, it will be time to leave the Net and make a site visit.

No wonder I feel so tired—
I'm older now than
I've ever been before.

It's not easy getting older, but there are some benefits to aging. Your children move out of the house. You can retire, relax, and look for new experiences and places to spend your money. Fortunately, many communities are recruiting seniors to relocate to their area.

Retirement community builders are looking for active retirees with annual incomes of at least $40,000 and a net worth of $325,000 who can pay their expenses when health problems arise. These communities are also recruiting businesses that complement them, such as banks, hospitals, research centers, real estate agencies, law firms, and assisted-housing developments. One community—Youngstown, Arizona,—has billed itself as the nation's first community intended specifically for retirees.

Sequim, Washington, has also successfully attracted retirees. Forty percent of the town's population is older than 65. Residents' financial and volunteer contributions have built excellent recreational facilities and a library, and brought in developers and medical specialists. They have also provided for the teenagers in the community by building a 25,000-square-foot gym and a Boys and Girls Club. Some senior residents have even started businesses.

Getting older no longer means that no one wants you. In fact, many retirees may be getting tired by enjoying all the benefits of a new location.

The best way to keep your kids out of hot water is to put some dishes in it.

Juveniles in the United States live in a much different world than their parents or grandparents. No longer are children being raised in a "Leave It to Beaver" household. Instead, they are more likely to follow in the footsteps of "Beavis and Butthead." Many lack motivation and have nowhere to go and nothing to do. More children live in poverty, teen-age birth has increased, fewer children are living in two-parent households, high school dropout rates are high, and drug use is more prevalent.

Problems experienced by children are the products of multiple, and sometimes complex, causes. One of the community's main goals should be to protect the public by creating a safe environment where kids can receive training, education, counseling, health care, art instruction, exercise, competitive sports, and outreach services. A top-quality before-school, after-school, or summer program can provide a safe place for kids and additional learning opportunities. At a time when more children are spending the hours between 2:00 and 6:00 p.m. unsupervised, the need for after-school programming is essential. Research shows that developing comprehensive after-school programs that are integrated into the regular school program and other family support systems within the community can yield positive results for students and their families.

Communities must prepare their youth to enter adulthood as contributing members of society. If they continue to ignore the importance and potential of this group, then the entire community will get burned.

A Purple Heart just proves that you were smart enough to think of a plan, stupid enough to try it, and lucky enough to survive.

Economic developers must have a thick skin that allows them to take their lumps and move on with projects in their community. The profession is highly visible and, therefore, one in which bumps, bruises, and welts are sure to be accumulated. The successful developer's secret is to move forward with a plan that is supported by the interests of the community. Involving the key stakeholders in plan development is one sure way to maximize its value to the community. These stakeholders are often defined as either community leaders or those who will be most impacted by the plan, or both.

Once the plan has been created, the developer must implement the plan in reasonable steps. Throughout the implementation process, the economic developer is almost guaranteed to incur some challenges along the way. It is at these points that their leadership capacity must shine the brightest.

If the plan was well prepared and implemented with leadership, the economic developer will be strengthened throughout the implementation process. As a result, the developer will qualify for the Medal of Honor, rather than the Purple Heart, for his or her contributions to the community.

Be like a duck:
keep calm and unruffled
on the surface,
but paddle like crazy underneath.

Work in the public sector can be stressful. Much of your work is conducted in public meetings and forums, and you don't have the luxury of hiding your mistakes. Successful practitioners make sure that obstacles are eliminated prior to opening their mouths at public meetings. Like the duck, what is seen on the surface has very little to do with what is going on underneath.

The truly great economic developers have the skids greased before they enter a meeting. They brief elected officials or board appointees on the project or proposal they intend to present prior to its introduction at the upcoming meeting. This can be time-consuming, but it is time well spent. No one likes to be shot down in public. Not only is it embarrassing, but repeated defeats destroy the economic developers' credibility.

By having "all their ducks in a row" prior to public debate, economic developers increase the number of their winning proposals substantially, and their reputation succeeds as well. Ask anyone who's been around for a while—it is much more fun to get approval votes than to play "duck and cover" in the public arena.

Living on Earth is expensive, but it does include a free trip around the sun.

The Cost of Living Index indicates that life is not getting cheaper. Housing, clothes, and food costs continue to rise while incomes often remain steady. After people pay all their bills, no money is left for a family vacation.

Economic developers focus on wage rates when they work to attract employers to their community. They try to bring jobs to the community that will raise the per capita income level and increase the tax base. This goal may not serve the best interest of the entire community.

There are many steps on the economic ladder. Call center or warehouse wage rates may not look like much on a community profile, but they mean a lot to those people who are moving up the ladder one step at a time. As Bill King, editor of *Expansion Management* magazine, points out, economic developers must remember that they represent the whole community and not just the higher income levels. Often, these jobs provide people with opportunities for better or secondary incomes.

Sometimes, what looks like a less than desirable job may enable a family to take a trip and enjoy more time in the sun.

Buy land.
They've stopped making it.

In the past, economic developers have been guilty of taking the easy way out (i.e., heading to the edge of town, grabbing 20 acres of land, and building a new industrial park). This method seemed to make sense, as zoning was easy to change and all the developer had to do to spur development was install water and sewer lines to new areas.

In the process, however, we left gaping holes in our communities where old, abandoned industrial or commercial sites sat vacant. We promoted urban sprawl when we needed to promote urban redevelopment. We traded smart growth for easy money. The costs have been substantial.

We quickly learned that the economic and social costs of urban sprawl soon surpassed the ease of developing at the urban fringe. There is no more land, but there are always new uses for the land that we have. When we focus on using the land we have, instead of expanding outward, our cups will run over with opportunity instead of our municipal boundaries overflowing with excessive costs of municipal operations.

All reports are in.
Life is now officially unfair.

Sometimes, no matter how hard you try, you always manage to come in second place. Another community always wins the economic development prize. The exit interviews indicate that your community had all the right assets, but, in the end, another community was chosen.

One way you can learn how to compete more effectively is to benchmark your community. Benchmarking—an important management and economic development tool—is the process of comparing your community with the competition.

Benchmarking forces a community to identify areas where it excels and where it lags. Benchmarking also enables a community to monitor its progress toward goals and measure its economic well-being through quantitative data that site selectors consider when selecting communities. Baseline Indicators, Economic Conditions Indicators, Economic Performance Indicators, and Capacity Indicators are the most common benchmarks.

Life may not be fair when it comes to economic development decisions, but a community that uses benchmarking learns how to compete more effectively.

If you can't get rid of the skeleton in your closet, you'd best teach it to dance.

— George Bernard Shaw

Let's face it: even Oz wasn't perfect. Every community has a blemish or two it would like to hide in the closet—and that's just the stuff that's on the surface. Hidden somewhere in many communities is that skeleton: the thing(s) you don't want anyone to know about. Eventually, people often do find out about the skeleton, and when they do, it has to come out.

In anticipation of such exposure, you must find ways to dress up the skeleton and make it dance. This is not lying; it's simply putting the best face possible on what could be a deal-killer piece of information. Even the worst skeleton has a good side, although admittedly some positive attributes take a little effort to find.

Make two lists about your skeleton: first, any positives that it may have, and second, what action plans are being implemented to correct the situation. Most prospects don't expect perfection; however, they do want to know that you're working on your problems. When you do teach your skeleton to dance, you'll find that the road for new investment gets smoother and easier to travel all the time.

Our childhood is what we spend the rest of our lives overcoming.

— AMY BENNET

It is an understatement to observe that people are interesting. They look to the future yet hold a strong foothold in the past. Many times the memories of even the smallest event can lead to a significant road block in their ability to partner on projects sometime in the future. Overcoming these hurdles can be essential for economic development to succeed.

For many of us, the senior homecoming football game creates memories of a date with that special someone, dinner, dancing and, with a little luck, a victory over the cross-town rival. As we reflect upon these memories, they remind us of the good times we had while growing up. However, these seemingly pleasant memories can turn economic development projects into nightmares as people try to resolve the loss that occurred twenty or more years ago.

Although the football game is used as an example, it represents a myriad of events that reflect how an event that happened many years in the past can fester and reel its head at some in opportune time in the future. When this does happen, the economic developer's job becomes more of a counselor than a technician. Sometimes, the path to success involves getting our leaders to act more like adults than children.

If you think no one cares about you, try missing a couple of payments.

While the sources of economic development financing can be many, the delivery typically comes in one of two forms: loans and grants.

An organization or business obtains a loan with the agreement that it will be paid back at a predetermined interest rate by a certain date. Businesses receive loans directly from such sources as the Small Business Administration (SBA), the United States Department of Agriculture (USDA) or Industrial Revenue Bonds (IRBs). Typically, these government-financing sources are able to provide longer terms, lower interest rates, and/or higher loan-to-value ratios than conventional lending sources. However, these loans must be paid back so they can stimulate economic development in other communities.

An organization may also receive a grant to financially support a program as specified in an approved proposal; the grant does not need to be repaid. Typically, grants are awarded to governments (cities, counties, states) or nonprofit organizations. Occasionally, the entity may be allowed to pass this grant money onto the private sector in exchange for meeting certain performance criteria, such as job creation, capital investment, or Brownfield redevelopment. The Community Development Block Grant (CDBG) program remains a favorite source.

Millions of dollars in loans and grant money are available each year. While the process is often extremely competitive—the loan or grant provider must identify the credit-worthiness of the borrower early in the lending process—loans and grants are important resources to improve our communities.

Volunteers are paid in six figures . . . SMILES.

—GAYLA LE MAIRE

Volunteers are dedicated people who believe in all work and no pay. They get paid by seeing the satisfaction on the faces of the people they help. Volunteers provide an essential service that may not otherwise be available. From the caring services provided by volunteers at hospitals to the busy parent coaching soccer or working with civic groups, volunteers are working every day. They are an important part of every community and are essential for a healthy community.

Volunteers also play a major role in economic development, serving on formal boards such as the Economic Development Commission (EDC) or the Workforce Investment Board (WIB), to sharing knowledge at small workshops. Communities rely on volunteers to improve the community and increase opportunities in the economic development arena.

Economic development organizations that use volunteers must realize that, although they are not paid staff, they must be trained as if they were. Volunteers are often the first to greet tourists, businesses, or site selectors who show an interest in an area. Therefore, they must be professional and knowledgeable in their work and attitude. The only thing worse than a trained volunteer who leaves is an untrained volunteer who stays.

The longer that an organization can keep a smile on a volunteer's face, the longer the volunteer will continue to accept a smile as payment for the work they do.

A thoughtful kid is one who leaves enough gas in the tank for you to get to the filling station.

The world of energy is quite volatile these days. If you don't believe this, look at what happened at the massive black-out that darkened much of the northeastern United States and Canada in August 2003. This volatility can provide true opportunities for those economic developers who are aware of the potential energy investment can provide.

Power is the most notable source of investment. As the electric grid deregulates the need to move power from source to consumption will expose the vulnerabilities in our system. This risk can be minimized as new, highly efficient power plants are built closer to consuming entities, which are frequently perceived as manufacturing facilities, but can also be hotels, drug stores, and hospitals. These power plants are quiet and expensive, which results in no impact on the community's quality of life yet an almost no-demand-for-service tax generating entity in the community.

Alternative energy sources are also presenting themselves as long-term lucrative investments. Areas with sustainable wind may be attractive for developing wind-generated power. Fuel cells, which will utilize natural gas and convert it to electricity, are being developed as well.

There is great economic opportunity on the horizon in the world of energy. Economic developers who keep an eye on them will find that the fuel tanks of their economic engines will be kept full.

The only time a windshield wiper works correctly is when it is holding a parking ticket.

Nothing will put a damper on a wonderful day of shopping and eating more quickly than a parking ticket. You probably have just spent a great deal of money in a downtown area and already paid a pretty penny in sales tax. You then walk out to your car and you see this white slip of paper on your windshield. You will think twice before you spend money in this area again.

Spokane, Washington, a community that understands the importance of visitor spending, will put a "ticket" under the windshield wiper of cars in violation of the parking limit. However, this is no typical ticket. It says:

> *Thanks for visiting downtown Spokane. While you were enjoying incredible shopping, world-class entertainment, the region's best dining, or professional services, your parking meter expired. Don't worry! This courtesy parking ticket extended your parking privileges another hour allowing you to enjoy your visit to Downtown Spokane.*

Communities must recognize that the road to increased revenues is marked with many tempting parking places. They will reap more money from dollars spent in existing businesses than they will with quarters in a meter.

Clones are people 2.

The good news: economic development has been tried and applied at many different levels through the years. Even better news: the best ideas tend to rise to the top. These ideas are shared by the leaders of the profession with the rising stars through training, certifications, and mentoring opportunities.

Economic developers who move into a community, especially into a new state, should learn who the best and brightest practitioners are in that state. Those people know how things work and how to get things done, and they have been through the development process. Their experience and wisdom can help the new economic developer to initiate a program quickly, professionally, and effectively.

The best news is that rarely do practitioners need to reinvent the wheel as they implement programs that meet the needs of the community they serve. By putting a team of mentors around their own program, they have the ability to clone the successful characteristics of others who can help solve their community's problems. Occasionally, this can be done with a cookie-cutter application of the principles, but often it requires minor alterations to increase the probability of success.

Sometimes you must take the test before you have finished studying.

Learning about economic development is a never-ending process. There are always new tools to discover, different strategies to implement, and new skills to acquire.

The International Economic Development Council (IEDC), the largest association of practitioners in the country, offers courses and workshops to help you stay skilled in the latest practices and issues in the profession. In addition, after you complete a series of classes and pass the required exams, it provides a certificate in economic development. Individuals who successfully complete the Certified Economic Developer program will be recognized as a CEcD. IEDC certification is a national recognition that increases your credibility in you current community and makes you more marketable for your next position.

The IEDC also coordinates an annual conference where thousands of practitioners come together and attend comprehensive educational sessions and hands-on tours of economic development. The IEDC offers the best networking in the country of community and economic development practitioners, industry experts, academicians, and government representatives.

As a practitioner committed to professional achievement, you must continually learn how to do your job better. The IEDC makes that task easier. After you pass all the IEDC tests, both you and your community will be better prepared for growth.

Minds are like parachutes — they only function when open.

— THOMAS DEWAR

People don't think about parachutes until they really need them. Then, if disaster strikes, they are glad someone made sure they were available. However, when disaster hits a community, are there parachutes available to make sure people will be safe? Risk management is one of the least talked about subjects in economic development, yet one of the most important.

The events of 9/11 taught us important lessons about why we need to pay more attention to known and suspected risks in our world. War and terrorism create enormous dangers for everyone. Our economy can be significantly stunted. This in turn reduces economic activity in nearly every American community.

Economic developers now must do a more thorough job of assessing known and suspected threats during the strategic planning process. Incentive investments in economic development projects must be evaluated more carefully for risks that could make deals fail in the short and long terms. Communities might want to hedge against economic risk by developing portfolios of incentive investments, industries, and jobs that assume that a certain number of projects are going to fail. Economic developers must work more closely and communicate more frequently with their clients and partners to respond to unexpected developments.

By better anticipating and managing risks affecting local economic development, we can be sure that our parachutes will open when our communities need them.

Mobile phones are the only subject on which men boast about who has the smallest.

— NEAL KINNOCK

Technology and economic development go hand in hand. The better the technology, the more productive the economic developer can be with the limited resources at hand. It is here that productivity has more to do with success than size.

Today, the most powerful tool of any economic development organization is its web page. Here, information about its product, the community, is portrayed in a proactive manner. The web page, of course, is accessed by computers, the majority of which are laptops in today's mobile economic development community. Combine that with a cell phone that is linked to a personal digital assistant (PDA), and you are one mobile set of hardware traveling about the community.

Successful economic development occurs as a result of multiple variables, many of which are supported by technology. Go ahead: get wired, get connected, and get as small as possible as you get on line.

As long as there are tests, there will be prayer in schools.

The Supreme Court has declared prayer in schools unconstitutional, yet millions of students start the day by saying, "Dear Lord, please let me pass this test." Now millions of parents will be praying that their children are able to pass tests, the results of which can determine whether students are promoted or graduate. With passage of the No Child Left Behind Act, standards, high-stakes testing, and accountability have become the policy frameworks within which schools in every state must operate.

Advocates tout high-stakes testing as a way to raise educational standards in school districts comprised mainly of poor, minority, and immigrant students. Many people, however, believe the policy has been shown to adversely affect the quality of education in these schools.

Regardless of whether the academic proficiency of students will be improved, increased use of testing in high school has become an economic development issue. More businesses are using high school testing scores as criteria for their business relocation decisions. States that have low test results will be eliminated from the site-selection decision at the outset.

Passing students through grades and awarding diplomas even if they do not achieve basic proficiency levels is unfair to the students, their families, and future employers. The consequences will become evident when they arrive at the workplace and lack the skills to succeed. By then, it will be too late to resort to prayer.

Love is grand.
Divorce is about a hundred grand.

Whoever said that parting is such sweet sorrow was never in economic development. There is no worse feeling than hearing that a business in your community has decided to leave. Sometimes the signs are evident for months or even years. At other times, you never see it coming. Not only will you feel as if you have lost a close friend, but your community will probably lose much in tax revenues, charitable giving, and leadership.

The relationship that a community has with each of its businesses is unique. Each of those relationships must be treated as a marriage. As your community's representative, you must communicate effectively with each business owner. Find out what is on her or his mind and what it will take to make them happy. You must keep your promises. You must be faithful to them and not covet their competition in another part of the country. You cannot take your businesses for granted.

Developing good communication, mutual respect, and appreciation are the foundation and most valuable outcomes of a business retention program. When these essentials of economic development are in place, both the community and the business will be richer and not poorer.

This is no ordinary silly grin on my face. It's an educated one.

The more you learn, the more you earn. The more education you have, the less chance that you will be unemployed. In a slow economy, those people with some education will get hired sooner than those without education.

Recent data shows that the estimated lifetime earnings of a high school graduate will be $686,850 while those without a high school degree will earn only $483,720. Further, if you have completed some college courses, you will earn $744,120. An associate degree will earn you $896,160 while a bachelor's degree will yield $1,214,340.

Education pays in part because employers believe educated workers learn tasks more easily and are better organized. They will pay more because they want to retain those workers. Those facts alone are reason to smile if your community can provide potential employers with an educated workforce.

The person who buys
the most lottery tickets
has the least chance of winning.

Many people think that entering the high-stakes world of business recruitment is like entering the lottery: the more tickets you buy, the better chance you have of winning. That is, the more companies that you pursue, the better chance that one of them will decide to locate in your area. However, just the reverse is true. The more companies you pursue, the least chance you have of being successful.

In order to increase the odds that a company will relocate to your community, you need to target industries. Targeting is the process of identifying an audience that has a need and high probability of responding positively to the promotion of a region, neighborhood, or other location. Economic development organizations should focus their time and money on industries that are most likely to have needs that a community can fill. Once an industry is targeted, then possible companies can be chosen from that list. You will have increased your odds by weeding out those companies that do not fit your profile.

The lottery and business attraction do have a number of things in common. Both are expensive and a gamble. However, if done right, business attraction offers the better long-term payback with a much higher probability of pay-off for the community.

When you do a good deed, get a receipt in case heaven is like the IRS.

Good record keeping and documentation is an important element in an economic development practitioner's toolbox. Most people do not realize all that a practitioner does—the demands of daily activities, the need to respond to requests from existing businesses and site selectors, completing critical projects, and attending numerous meetings. Economic development cannot be measured by just the number of jobs that are added to a community. Documentation shows the myriad of activities completed by the practitioner and could be used to support a larger budget or additional help.

Documentation is also especially important when working with prospects so that there is no misunderstanding when delicate negotiations take place. Business attraction activities occur over a long period of time. Meetings and promises are easily forgotten. Documentation provides a history and reminder of the prospect's visits and conversations.

The number one reason why most practitioners say they don't document is because they don't have time. Documentation usually gets ignored and placed in the "to do later" file. Unfortunately, the next day is much the same and the documentation gets further and further behind.

Practitioners accomplish good work in a community. But much of that work never gets noticed. Documentation may not get you into heaven, but it may save your job and reap many more benefits.

When you stretch the truth, watch out for the snapback.

— BILL COPELAND

The competitive advantage in economic development comes from three things: sustained investment in infrastructure, accurate and truthful information, and rapid delivery. While all three are essential for success, honesty—or the lack thereof—can bring a development program to its knees in an instant.

Case in point: A Midwest economic developer, while filling out one of those infamous 20-page questionnaires that need to be completed within 24 hours, entered a value of 70 psi for the community's water distribution system at the proposed site.

The developer returned the questionnaire, and eventually the community was selected for the new food processing plant. Press conferences involving the mayor and governor followed, and a ground-breaking ceremony was held. Soon construction crews were putting in footings for the new facility. Then the site engineer checked system pressure in the feed lines from the water treatment plant. He couldn't believe his readings of 20 psi! Phone calls led to meetings that went all the way to the State Department of Commerce. Threats of lawsuits for fraud were insinuated, and many people became very nervous.

The State made a quick decision: a new water storage tank would be built at the site in order to help the business locate in the community. Sure, the economic developer won the project. However, future projects were not to be had for that community, as long as that economic developer remained. Stretching the truth paid off for this individual, but the ramifications cost the community consideration for additional projects for many years.

I was told to pay my taxes with a smile but they still wanted money.

While one is really happy about paying taxes, taxes provide the services required by a society's citizens. These services include maintaining parks and roads, providing security, and educating children. These services are called community development.

Reasonable taxes are the price of civilization. You are not just paying taxes; you are investing in the future of your community.

Most of us recognize that our economy is more productive with a prudent level of public goods and services than with none at all. The cost must be paid somehow. A society in which most citizens pay their taxes usually produces more goods and services than societies in which tax evasion is rampant and government must spend inordinate amounts of money to collect taxes.

No tax system is perfect. But rather than think about how much you are paying, think about the services you and your children receive. At least your children will smile for what you leave for them in the future.

Isn't it strange?
The same people who laugh at gypsy fortunetellers take economists seriously.

Thankfully, no one has ever connected economic impact analysis with fortunetelling. Most people would hold economists in some light of credibility and put fortunetellers under scrutiny. But isn't fortunetelling what economic-impact analysis really is? We are quantifying the good fortunes of the community as we decide to package or encourage a potential project.

Economic-impact analysis allows the community to quantify the costs and benefits associated with growth and to assess them in a concise, efficient manner. The spreadsheets become the palms that are read by the soothsayers who analyze the practitioner's efforts. The future is forecasted based upon actions of the past and present. The economic-impact analysis effort peers into the analyst's crystal ball to predict the outcome of the new investment. All involved hope that the new project will bring good fortune to the community.

The community takes economists' reports seriously. If based upon facts and high-quality data, the reports help guide decision makers' efforts. When deals close, they typically result in good fortune for the community receiving the investment. Upon reflection, economists and fortunetellers do have more in common than previously thought.

Lead me not into temptation.
I can find the way myself.

In the movie *The Graduate*, Benjamin Braddock returns from college and is approached by a family friend. The friend puts his arm around Benjamin and says one word: "Plastics."

Today, communities are putting their arms around another industry: "biotech." Hundreds of cities are hoping to become the next hotbed for this industry. A recent survey conducted by the U.S. Department of Commerce indicated that more than 80 percent of the responding states and municipalities listed biotech as one of their top two targets for development. They are being tempted by the allure of high-paying jobs and the prospect that biotech companies will follow one another.

While most practitioners agree that biotech will be around for awhile, the benefits of such a company may not be worth the effort that is required to attract one. First, the numbers of jobs in this field are relatively small—only 180,000 jobs nationwide. Most companies employ fewer than 25 employees, and only a handful of companies make money. Studies have shown that it takes an average of about 15 years for a biotech company to turn a profit, if it can stay in business that long. Currently, the industry's overall losses are nearly $6 billion.

As for the idea that biotech companies follow one another, that is very true. But breaking into this group is nearly impossible. The top five biotech clusters—Boston, San Francisco, San Diego, Seattle, and Raleigh-Durham—account for three-fourths of the biotech venture capital. Knowing this, you may be tempted to pursue the path of a more prosperous industry.

Lottery: A tax on people who are bad at math.

— ALEX PETTY

STATE LOTTO

KACHING

I'VE GOT A ONE AND GAZILLION CHANCE of WINNING? I'LL TAKE IT!!

One does not generally play the lottery because the odds are in their favor. In fact, the odds are stacked strongly against those people who purchase tickets. Yet, someone invariably wins. In some states, with every ticket sold, there are many winners because lottery profits go directly to pay for community and economic development services.

Oregon is one state whose constitution mandates that money go specifically for public schools, businesses, workforce, state parks, and salmon protection. The Oregon State Lottery's purpose is to provide additional revenue to those public purposes without the imposition of additional increased taxes. The Oregon State Lottery is entirely self-financed through its sales and does not receive any General Fund or other tax dollars.

Since the lottery began in 1985, more than $3.4 billion in lottery profits has gone to public education and economic development programs throughout Oregon. During that same time, players have won more than $8.3 billion in prizes, and almost $2 billion has been paid to Oregon businesses for services and supplies needed to operate the lottery.

As long as people can play the lottery, they can dream about the way their life could change. For many others, the lottery is changing their life on a daily basis without even playing.

A library should be the delivery room for the birth of ideas.

— Norman Cousins

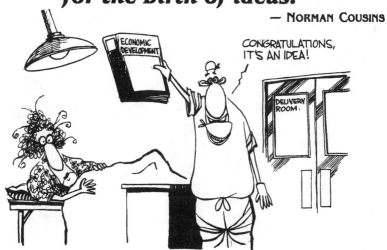

For years, libraries were places for finding books or sleeping. The books were free and the environment was quiet. Now that we have moved into the information age, libraries have become an important institution to attract and retain businesses. Community support of libraries has recently appeared on quality-of-life criteria for businesses interested in relocating.

Successful libraries demonstrate their role in the economic development arena through their policies and services and in the efforts of their staff to promote the community. They are especially important in rural communities where access to global information will put those areas on an equal level with their competitors in urban areas. Librarians can help locate demographic information used for recruiting, monitoring local business trends, and finding grants and loans.

Libraries also encourage community development, as they offer meeting places to promote and stimulate culture and to share ideas. Besides being centers where many points of view are available in books, community leaders can meet in libraries to discuss issues and strategically plan for their communities, or hold receptions for existing and new businesses.

Communities all over the country, large and small, from Nashville, Tennessee, to Lodi, Ohio, are building new libraries—places to find books as well as ideas. They help people connect when they are awake, as well as provide a comfortable place to dream about your community's future.

No member of a crew is praised for the rugged individuality of his rowing.

— RALPH WALDO EMERSON

Once upon a time, it was sufficient to build an economic development team that included just local stakeholders who were immediately involved in our work. Today, globalization forces all of us out of our "local box."

Globalization is sparking much greater competition for economic development opportunities. Companies and industries have built global operations, creating vast and far-reaching worldwide webs in which they conduct business. India, China, Singapore, and many other developing nations are gearing up as new centers for the emerging knowledge economy. The economic fate of communities worldwide is becoming much more interlocked as globalization thrusts them together. Companies like Microsoft and General Motors now rely on vast global networks of places to support and sustain their businesses.

What does all this mean for economic development? New collaborative partnerships will need to be built on a national and international basis with other Economic Development Organizations (EDOs). Communities which ordinarily defined themselves as competitors must learn to collaborate with each other to create new economic opportunities for their areas. If they have the same companies and industries, they have a vested interest in forming "community supplier networks" and using other tools to help them develop mutually beneficial opportunities.

Strategic relationship building will be a core competency for EDOs worldwide in the not too distant future. We will either row the boat collectively or we will drown individually.

If you lined up all the cars in the world end to end, someone would still be stupid enough to try and pass them.

One of the big challenges in economic development is the community's ability to effectively move people and goods. Communities that understand this issue address it early and often in their growth management strategies. Those that fail to do so end up with traffic congestion as far as the eye can see.

When a community is unable to move goods and people from one place to another, it is doomed to stay where it is: stationary on the economic highway of growth. When that happens, other communities pass it, leaving it in a cloud of dust. The issue isn't just about where to build a highway or rail system; it is also about what effects it will have. Will it alter land use patterns or cause congestion of urban transportation or urban sprawl? How will it encourage economic growth?

Transportation has taken a front seat in shaping economic development strategies and policies nationwide. Besides the inherent value of increased mobility, individuals may benefit from increased employment options as their range of safe, feasible commuting is expanded. Businesses may then able to choose from a larger supply of labor as more potential employees fall within their commuting range. Transportation improvements can also decrease the cost of doing business.

Wise transportation investments and economic development are mutually reinforcing processes. Where highways, buses, and trains efficiently move people and goods, economic growth occurs. Don't let it pass you by.

A school: a building with four walls and tomorrow inside.

Children are the key to a better future. They will be tomorrow's teachers, doctors, scientists, parents, and presidents. We must invest in our schools to make sure children get the best education possible. A good education is the most significant predictor of a good lifestyle; it is also the engine that drives economic development and makes other things possible in a community.

The entire community can support our schools in various ways: voting for school levies that help reduce class size, building more schools, and providing state-of-the-art equipment. The hidden costs of poorly subsidized schools are higher unemployment and higher rates of crime and incarceration.

One unique form of support for schools is Teach for America. This New York–based organization, funded by AmeriCorps, operates much like the Peace Corps and places people in 18 locations around the country. It recruits recent college graduates from the nation's top universities to serve two-year stints at poor school districts. Once immersed in the program, they become advocates in support of high-quality education for all children. These community leaders serve as positive role models for children, and they also gain a deeper understanding of the importance of education, especially in depressed and struggling districts. Since its inception in 1990, approximately 9,000 individuals have joined Teach For America. More than 1.25 million students have benefited from the program.

When it comes down to investing in our schools, educating adults will be our children's best hope for tomorrow.

Doesn't "expecting the unexpected" make the unexpected expected?

Whenever successful economic developers enter a deal negotiation, board meeting, or council presentation, they prepare by defining all the possible outcomes of the event. They either manage expectations early on or prepare the participants prior to the meeting. As a result, they are able to focus on three different outcomes:

Best-Case Scenario: What would happen if you were to get everything you wanted. When this happens, everyone is on board, you've done your homework, and you've briefed the decision-makers prior to the event.

Most Probable Outcome: What you anticipated to happen prior to the meeting. After knowing all the facts and the players, the successful economic developer can pretty much determine what is going to come out of the meeting.

Fall Back Position: Not even the best developers succeed every time. However, when they enter into negotiations they know what they'd like to accomplish (Best Case Scenario), and what is most likely to occur (Most Probable Outcome). They also have a contingency plan—the Fall Back Position—in place in case the meeting blows up on them.

Surprises work best at birthday parties and Christmas, not at economic development events. Your goal as an economic developer is to minimize the surprises.

Ugly plants grow much faster than beautiful ones.

In 1989, the city of Littleton, Colorado, worked with the Center for the New West in taking a new approach to economic development: "economic gardening." Rather than focusing on recruiting "beautiful" companies from outside the area, their goal was to create nurturing environments for growth companies in their own communities. Although working with existing companies is often referred to as the "ugly" part of economic development, the local government realized that by assisting local businesses, they would create a more competitive environment, produce additional jobs, and become a more prosperous community.

The government assists local businesses in several ways: by providing sophisticated tools of information, making connections with mutually related service providers, and maintaining basic infrastructure (streets, water and sewer), quality of life infrastructure (parks and art) and intellectual infrastructure (schools, training and telecommunications). Since the inception of the program, job growth has gone from 16,000 to 24,000 without recruiting one company. Sales taxes have grown from $5 million to more than $16 million. Littleton is one of the few cities that is pondering how to spend its excess revenues.

Many communities—both nationwide and internationally—are developing and implementing economic gardening programs. (See the web site of California State University Center for Economic Development in Chico for a list: *http://www.csuchico. edu/cedp/biap/econ.gardening.html*.) These communities have shown that the "ugly" companies will grow faster than the "beautiful" ones. Support your local plants.

Just because you are trained for something doesn't mean you are prepared for it.

In conventional management development, training is training and doing is doing, and never the twain shall meet. It is one thing to learn how to read a particular recipe, but until the food is actually prepared and tasted, you may want to resist cooking it when the boss comes for dinner. Human performance can be greatly enhanced if training methods are changed to reflect real-life situations. Training is best when skills are developed to meet a company's current and future needs and to awaken people to their intellectual and artistic strengths and weaknesses.

One of the most successful job training models in the United States is FareStart *(www.farestart.org)* in Seattle, Washington. This nonprofit organization helps homeless and disadvantaged men and women through job training and placement in the food service industry. For the past ten years, FareStart has provided more than 800,000 meals and has transformed more than 1,000 lives through their innovative and extensive Learning for Life Program.

At FareStart, food is the tool that empowers lives, nourishes families, and builds communities. While still living in Seattle's homeless shelters, students show up to work every weekday on time, clean, sober, appropriately dressed, and ready to learn and work. After completing the 16-week program, they discover that in addition to the courage that brought them to FareStart, they now have a marketable skill, tools for life, a place of belonging in the community, and the opportunity for a successful future.

Life is like wrestling a gorilla.
You don't stop when you get tired.
You stop when the gorilla gets tired.

— ROBERT STRAUSS

Working with site selectors and consultants has a beginning and an end. The problem is that you don't usually know the time frame between the two. Certainly the time frame for relocations has been shortened as a result of technology. During the last 15 years, the decision time has been cut in half. A company is typically anxious to shorten the decision-making process so it can relocate quickly and start making money in its new location. Many projects are now being decided within six to eight weeks.

However, communities are rarely in control of when the final decisions are made. They work within the prospect's time frame, not their own. This is why requests for information come in spurts. Information is sought as soon as it is needed. The time frame is always *now*. You and your team may work day and night in order to meet the deadline. With each new deadline it meets, the community's expectation that a decision is forth-coming increases.

Weeks pass before the community hears from the company, and then it is with a request for more information—immediately. This is when you can't quit. You return to your office and keep wrestling with data, maps, and charts. You know that sometime soon, the gorilla will get tired and a decision will be made. If you have done your job, your community will be the winner.

Just because love is blind doesn't mean your web site should be.

— MARK JAMES

In order to find the love of your life, you need to be in the right place at the right time. There is no faster way to find love at first site than on the Internet. Communities that wish to be found must make sure that the right clicks lead right to them. You never know when an entrepreneur will be looking for a location to start or grow their business. Branding your site and directly marketing it to potential visitors through search engines can accomplish this.

First, branding your site starts with naming it. Some creative people have developed URLs (registered domain names) such as *locatein(thisplace)*, or *doingbizin(thisplace)*. Once named, no piece of letterhead paper, business card, promotional item or marketing piece should leave the office without the web site address included.

Second, how you are found by the search engines is also critical. The best search engines have indexed (listed) only 35 percent of the sites available. A practitioner's job is to make sure search engines find and index the community site properly. This can be accomplished by submitting your site to search engines. Take a look at *www.searchenginewatch.com* for a wealth of information on search engines.

Finding the love of your life should take time. Finding the right community can be quick. Communities should make sure their site will be found in all the right places.

Some people are like Slinkies . . . you can't help but smile when you see one tumble down the stairs.

Most economic developers have integrity and are professional when they compete for companies. However, some people prefer to take the low road. They criticize the competition, misrepresent comparative data, and spread rumors about their neighbors.

When marketing your community, be positive. Focus on what the community offers, not on what the competition cannot do. During the California energy crisis, some communities chose to make light of California's crisis and poked fun at them in hopes of stealing businesses. Even during the 9/11 disaster, some people targeted New York companies, urging them to leave and relocate to a safer community.

Marketing campaigns that use fear and insensitivity do not have a place in this profession. Not only will they more than likely fail in recruiting those companies, but also they will rarely succeed in attaining economic development goals. As a result, those communities will soon start to tumble and never find the stairs leading to economic growth.

Stupidity is not considered a handicap. Park elsewhere.

There is nothing more wonderful than finding a parking place right in front of the store where you want to shop. Not only do you feel lucky, but you also feel so good that it makes you want to spend more money. Yet many employers allow their own employees to park in the closest parking spots, which discourage people from shopping at their store. Even though convenient customer parking relates to a more profitable business (and, hence, job security), the city often ends up enforcing an arbitrary deadline.

Towns usually post two-hour parking limits to discourage retail employees from hogging the best parking spaces for the eight hours they are at work. In solving one problem, they create another. Most studies have shown that shoppers, especially ones from out of town, need about four hours to satisfy their purchasing needs. Visitors who are forced to keep watching the time usually leave before they complete their shopping. Rarely will visitors go out, move the car to another location, and then return to continue breaking out the plastic. They will just leave.

Shopping and dining in a pedestrian setting is one of the most popular visitor activities and generates a great deal of revenue for a community. Wise employers don't handicap shoppers by letting their employees to take the best parking spaces.

Happiness comes through doors you didn't know you left open.

In economic development, don't close any doors behind you. Communities typically consider exports to be good for the economy and imports to be the cause of lost jobs. Consequently, they do not cater to the small foreign firm needing help to establish a sales office. After all, what could such firm do for the community?

Communities often forget that companies like to test markets with small ventures before diving in headfirst. What looks like a small sales office today could be the next Honda or Toyota of tomorrow. A community has a better chance of developing strong relationships with the small foreign firms exploring the U.S. market than with the international conglomerates. Also, everyone else is chasing the large firms.

Look for companies headquartered in countries with similar wage rates and/or high product transportation costs. These types of companies will have the highest probability of growing into U.S. manufacturing plants. Over the long term, developing and maintaining relationships with small international companies will keep the door open for the community to be selected when the company grows up.

Everyone has the ability to make someone happy, some by entering the room and others by leaving it.

Economic development organizations go through a touchy process as they select (or receive) members who will sit on their boards. Often, the individuals most interested in being on the board are not the same as those who will bring the most value to the table. Board member selection is neither a simple nor a laissez-faire process, but it needs to appear that way in the public arena.

A successful economic development program has an ongoing succession process in place. The developer must make sure that the appropriate organizations are represented on the board and that the best and brightest people on those boards are selected for membership on the EDC. The accomplishment of this process is not happenstance. The developer must continually observe, discuss, and select the most valuable members to be included on the board of directors.

The developer must make sure that when EDC members enter the room, those in attendance are happy they came. If the smiles occur when they leave, your program credibility will be leaving the community at the same time.

The two best times to keep your mouth shut are when you're swimming and when you're angry.

We all say things we wish we could take back. When you are dealing with friends, they will often understand and let it slide. But in economic development, as in any profession, showing your anger in a public session can have serious consequences.

One community learned this lesson the hard way. As a "one-horse town," the community was overly dependent on one company for jobs and taxes. The company was undergoing difficult times and had asked local leaders for some incentives that would help them manage their challenges better. The soft economy was creating stress on the city council also. Rather than working with the company to assist them, one elected official started complaining about how much the company had already received from the city. He wondered aloud how this company had the nerve to ask for more when the city had already helped them in so many other ways in the past. Others in the community became angry with the company as well.

The company eventually decided it was no longer wanted in the community. Within months, it started the process of closing the plant by laying off people and moving the remaining jobs elsewhere. This community has still not recovered and now has one of the highest unemployment rates in the state. All this because one person got angry, could not keep his mouth shut, and refused to help the company return to the swim of things.

Unfortunately, we are not equipped with hindsight in advance.

Land has always been one of the most important commodities in economic development. Practitioners, in their quest to build capacity in their communities, often look at the edge of town as the place to build a new industrial park to lure prospects. Unfortunately, in their zeal to attract a business, they may ignore existing sites in town, many of which are brownfields.

Brownfield sites are properties which may include the presence or potential presence of a hazardous substance, pollutant, or contaminant. In the United States, there are about 650,000 sites, comprising more than 3.2 million acres of land. Economists estimate that by allowing these parcels to sit vacant, we are losing out on the creation of 3.7 million jobs and more than $2 billion in tax revenue.

The Brownfield Economic Redevelopment Initiative empowers states, communities, and other stakeholders involved in the environment and economic development to work together to safely clean up and redevelop brownfield sites. The Thea Foss redevelopment in Tacoma, Washington, is a showcase for successful brownfield redevelopment. The reclaimed site is now home to retail stores, restaurants, urban housing, and the Museum of Glass, featuring art by Tacoma native Dale Chihuly.

When we learn to look at our brownfields as assets, we can see the value of properties located within town.

A banker is a person who is willing to make a loan if you present sufficient evidence to show you don't need it.

— HERBERT PROCHNOW

Lack of financing for the earliest stages of business development is one of the biggest barriers to creating job growth in a community. Banks, often seen as traditional sources of funding, may not be amenable to funding the early stages of a venture.

Banks, however, are not the only source for raising money for economic development. Professional investors provide venture capital to support young, rapidly growing companies that have the potential to develop into successful businesses and economic contributors to your community. Venture capitalists regularly invest in companies with the potential for a high rate of return within three to five years. Many professionally managed venture capital firms exist as private partnerships, closely held corporations, or as private individuals.

Working with venture capitalists, though, may not be for the independent entrepreneur. In addition to expecting a high rate of return, venture capitalists may also require representation on the company board and demand some control over how the company is managed. Having an outsider exert control is often an anathema to many entrepreneurs.

On the other hand, an entrepreneur may have a hard time turning down venture capital. Bank financing requires evidence that you can pay back a loan. Venture capitalists require that you have a good idea and the ability to make it happen.

He uses statistics as a drunken man uses lampposts . . . for support rather than for illumination.

— ANDREW LANG

Communities that are serious about competing for the economic dollar must use statistics to put themselves in the best light. Statistics provide the only way that site selectors and businesses can fairly compare their criteria.

The two best sources that detail the data to be collected are the *Site Selection Handbook for Communities,* published by the International Economic Development Council, and *So You Want to be on a Short List,* by Audrey Taylor of Chabin Concepts. These excellent publications help economic developers better understand the highly competitive process of site selection and provide a list of the data resources most used by site selectors.

Data needs to be readily available and timely so that the community can respond quickly and completely to an investment prospect's requests. Compiling data on economic and industrial changes and emerging jobs also helps the community understand itself.

When the practitioner charts statistics and evaluates the relevancy of current development programs to future business needs, he or she develops support for the community's claims of being the best place for a business to locate. This information shines light on a community's assets and can boost the argument for why their community should be considered for the short list of business relocation contenders. Of course, this only works if the community illuminates the right statistics.

To invent, you need a
good imagination and a pile of junk.

— THOMAS EDISON

When we were children, we had great imaginations. A sandbox could become a castle, a swing could become an airplane, and a watch could be a time machine. If you looked back at the childhoods of some great inventors, you would discover there was some object that may have looked like junk to most adults, yet it became a metaphor for their life's work. As many of us grow up, we lose that ability to combine our imagination with some object and transform it into something entirely different, useful, and fun.

Inventors are an important part of the entrepreneurial spirit that has become essential in economic development. Economic developers can play a contributing role in the development process of the inventor. In order to do that, the practitioner needs to play three different roles. They need to be like the inventor and be a dreamer, a realist, and a critic. The dreamer will be able to see the potential of the idea, the realist will figure out how to bring the product to market and provide financing, and the critic will need to be honest with the inventor and determine if demand exists for the dream.

Many inventors have little business savvy. Therefore, the developer must recognize and assist those people who have not lost their ability to imagine like a child in hopes that they can turn junk into gold for the community.

Money is something you must have in case you don't die young.

ECONOMIC MATH

GRAYS HARBOR TOURISM + GRAY HAIR = GREEN

The average life expectancy for people is 76.9 years—almost double what it was 200 years ago. People are living increasingly longer lives, and reaching 100 will soon be commonplace.

Almost 60 million Americans, or about 28 percent of the adult population, are at least 55 years of age. They are more active, health conscious, activity driven, and independent than previous generations. They also have the money to pursue more activities. The travel industry estimates that this group accounts for $130 billion in travel spending and takes one third of all trips defined as journeys of 50 miles or more. Communities are missing out on a tremendous niche market in tourism if they do not appeal to the over-55 generation.

To rekindle growth in the travel market, communities are developing programs and strategies to attract the mature citizen. Grays Harbor County, Washington, has targeted the older tourists by offering nature walks, bird watching, canoeing, storm watching, and beach combing. This community believes that these activities will provide mature tourists with exercise, romance, fun, and the desire to spend their children's inheritance.

It is far more impressive when others discover your good qualities without your help.

When you were in high school and wanted someone to notice you, a good plan was to have a friend extol your good points. Usually, the plan worked and it was then your responsibility to prove that your friend was a credible matchmaker. Getting noticed in economic development works much the same way.

Public relations—a very big part of every community marketing program—differs from advertising. Advertising is what you do. Public relations is what someone else does for you. Studies have shown that 10 percent of the U.S. population makes decisions based on ads they see, 40 percent as a result of an article they have read and 50 percent because of recommendations from colleagues and friends. Though no corporate relocation will take place as a result of any of these, understanding these tools will help you get noticed.

Articles that are strategically placed by third parties lend great credibility to your marketing efforts. They are more likely to be read than paid ads. They have also proven to yield a better return on a community's investment than other forms of marketing. Many full-page ads cost an enormous amount while the cost of using a public relations firm pales in comparison. Some studies have shown that $3 of publicity is attained for every $1 spent on a public relations campaign.

Most relationships—business and personal—are brought together as a result of a third party. Let someone else brag about your community's strengths,and you may start a relationship with a business that will last a lifetime.

Computers make very fast, very accurate mistakes.

Technology—including cell phones, computers and web pages —is a strong part of economic development. The speed with which technology can accelerate information dissemination or decision-making is impressive. Yet technology can also amplify mistakes at the same speed.

Every piece of information must be entered correctly, and edits must be made carefully. To be sure that information released to the public is accurate, an economic developer should:

1) Plan ahead to prevent time compression as deadlines near;
2) Ask a skilled editor to proof documents prior to release;
3) Ask an accountant to audit spreadsheets prior to release; and,
4) Separate data input on spreadsheets into "assumptions" pages and protect the remaining pages from editing.

An economic developer has an advantage when he or she provides accurate data and quick responses. Successful organizations build into their work plan the methods that minimize the opportunity for failure. The computer is only as good as the user. What are you doing to improve the accuracy of your work this week?

Having a green thumb does not necessarily make you a good gardener; you could simply be a lousy painter.

Many communities have business retention programs. Economic development practitioners survey their businesses on a regular basis. They sit down with business owners to find out what is on their minds. They try to find warning signs that will reveal when a company is in danger of closing or relocating.

Having a business retention program, however, does not necessarily mean you will retain companies. Too many retention programs only provide emotional, empathetic, or networking support. They may produce numerous reports with pie charts and graphs, but those don't usually help the community retain its businesses or determine when they are ready to expand.

Eric Canada of Blane, Canada Ltd. has successfully moved from a process-driven style of retention and expansion to a portfolio-management model. This model provides a deeper understanding of each company to determine how it fits in the community's economic future. His comprehensive survey collects information that focuses on value to the community, growth potential, technological adaptation, risk of downsizing, and satisfaction with the community.

Calling a business survey a business-retention program does not necessarily make it so. The goal should be to grow your companies by implementing policies and programs that form the environment where they can thrive. Only then will a community become a fertile garden of business growth.

Stealing ideas from one person is plagiarism; stealing from many is research.

It seems as if there are never any new ideas in economic development. Instead, practitioners are merely refining strategies that have been around for decades. Therefore, you can never underestimate the value of good researchers in your community.

Good researchers will help economic development organizations become efficient in recruiting companies and retaining businesses. They can track down companies interested in relocating and help existing businesses follow trends that can keep them ahead of the curve. Researchers produce comprehensive reports that put them in the forefront of a site selector's mind, and they mail information relevant to policy makers in identifying the cost of doing business.

Economic development researchers often say that they just got five to ten. What that means is they just uncovered five to ten great ideas that will result in five to ten years of economic growth.

A knowledge economy does not just refer to jobs being created in the technology field. It also refers to people who know how to retrieve information that is beneficial to a community. Good research is an important tool in a community's growth.

All of us could take a lesson from the weather. It pays no attention to criticism.

Many communities have discovered which way the wind is blowing and have decided to support environmentally friendly energy resources, such as wind and solar. The recent energy crisis and power blackouts, as well as increased criticism of the more traditional hydroelectric and fossil fuel sources, have refueled the interest in new sources of affordable energy.

Wind farms are becoming popular not only because they are a clean source of energy but also because they can create jobs and increase the tax base in a community. A proposed wind farm in Ellensburg, Washington, is projected to create about 185 full-time jobs and add $16 million in income to the county. New technology has offered new ways to minimize environmental concerns on surrounding areas. Certain tax credits are available that make it competitive with natural gas.

The American Wind Energy Association recently reported that the United States lags behind Europe in wind installations. The U.S. ranks third in international wind-generated power production but has less than half the total capacity of number one–ranked Germany. Overall, the U.S. produces 15 percent of wind power, while Europe accounts for 75 percent.

Economic development should balance the needs of economic growth with environmental protection. Mother Earth often provides us with the answer to our needs. If only communities can be wise enough to stop criticizing her and listen, they will discover that they can have both.

A consultant is someone who comes in to solve a problem and stays around long enough to become part of it.

In economic development, communities have resorted to hiring consultants to help them with a vast array of activities. Part of the reason is that they are unable to hire full-time employees because they don't have a position available but they have the money. Consultants bring experience to the table that communities often lack. They have been though the process of raising funds, recruiting a company, or developing strategic plans. To some, an outsider is always better than someone from the area.

In order to maximize the probability that your consultant will become part of the solution, remember that the relationship between you and your consultant should be collaborative. One of the biggest mistakes communities often make is expecting a consultant to relieve them of all responsibility in a project. This is your community and your project, so you need to be involved and retain responsibility for it. It cannot be shifted entirely to a consultant. Conversely, be wary of a consultant who is reluctant to accept community input. The time line and work scope for any project should clearly incorporate specific points in the process for review, discussion, and buy-in by local decision makers. Be sure that your consultant is prepared to present project information, answer questions, and incorporate public comments, as appropriate. With proper direction, a consultant can be part of the solution, rather than the problem.

If you ever think you are too small to be effective, you've never been to bed with a mosquito.

— BETTY REESE

Despite the fact that many rural communities have a lot to offer relocating companies, their access to financial markets is limited. In fact, 87 percent of venture capitol ends up in the larger metropolitan areas. A new program by the Washington Technology Center and the U.S. Department of Commerce will soon provide some smaller communities with greater effectiveness in their efforts to attract new industries and jobs.

The two agencies have joined forces to organize investment groups and create a statewide network of wealthy individuals whose goal is to ignite business development in rural regions. If successful, the program will help create jobs and new industries in areas where forestry, fishing, and farming are in decline. Money will be used to set up investment networks and entrepreneurial classes in six to eight communities around the state.

A mosquito proves its effectiveness through pure determination. It has a continued drive toward accomplishment and a genetic predisposition for survival. Communities with the same predisposition for survival will find that their effectiveness comes from matching the resources available with the entrepreneurs that turn them into job-creating businesses. As the mosquito well knows, size does not matter.

Money isn't everything, but it sure keeps you in touch with your children.

Once you introduce money to children, a new relationship emerges. The Ewing Marion Kauffman Foundation has been introducing the excitement and opportunity of youth entrepreneurship to thousands of children between the ages of five and 18. They have been very successful working with colleges, universities, school districts, and youth organizations to train educators and facilitators to show them how work makes an impact on society. Their focus is to introduce young people to the rewards of "making a job" rather than "taking a job."

One of the foundation's latest ventures is collaboration with Disney Online on a game called "Hot Shot Business." This interactive game shows youth how to establish and run their own businesses. In a town called Opportunity City, two animated teenage characters help players understand their neighborhood needs by walking them though financing, partnerships, marketing, bookkeeping, and other small business activities.

Youth entrepreneurship programs are the stepping stone to creating future businesses in your community. Recent surveys show that seven out of 10 high school students reported wanting to start their own businesses. Six in 10 youth said that they would rather own a small business than work for a large corporation. Interestingly, students reported the major reason for wanting to start their own business was not the opportunity to make large amounts of money, but the desire to gain personal independence. With that many children wanting to become entrepreneurs, it won't be long before you stay in touch with your children by asking them if you can borrow money.

There is no reason why clothes must match.

Wearing clothes that do not match is a sign of creativity and eccentricity. In the past, we were taught to avoid these people. Yet, one of the most talked-about books in economic development states that communities should embrace people who are creative and eccentric. These people catch the attention of high-tech industries and spur economic growth.

Richard Florida, in *The Rise of the Creative Class*, writes about the great value in tapping into the creative community. Florida's work indicates a direct correlation between diversity and creativity with regional growth. In fact, it is a more reliable gauge than some of the conventional measures used to determine why an industry moves to a particular location. Florida measures the three T's of economic development: technology, talent, and tolerance. For a community to be successful, it must have all three of these in order to generate innovation and stimulate economic activity. Florida's premise seems to hold true, as the cities that rank high on the creativity list are San Francisco, Austin, Boston, and San Diego. These same cities are national leaders at attracting high-tech companies.

The lesson in this is that the most ordinary things can initiate prosperity in a community. "Cities need a people climate even before they need a business climate," said Florida. Communities should start embracing and recruiting diverse individuals, even if their clothes do not match.

Some people work up steam and some only generate fog.

In economic development, there is a huge difference between "activity" and "productivity." Understanding that difference is essential to the long-term success of an economic developer's career.

Due to the high-profile nature of economic development, local practitioners are commonly asked to serve on many boards and commissions in their communities. Over time, their schedule fills with unending meetings but few accomplishments. They are busy, but their reason for existence often gets lost in the fog of busy-ness.

Others stay focused on their job responsibilities. They participate in those meetings and task forces that will bear fruit for their goals and objectives. As they work, they produce results, exude passion, and motivate others to be productive.

The challenge in economic development is to separate productivity from activity. The goal is to heat things up in the local economy and generate the steam for the community's economic engines. As these engines roar to life, the fog of indecision and ineffectiveness is cleared.

There are more ways to do something wrong than there are ways to do it right.

When we were young and in school, it was okay to make mistakes. Rarely were the results of our mistakes life-altering or threatening. But as we grow older, we discover that some of the mistakes made in the name of economic development can be devastating. People often lose their jobs when companies close. The effects on families and communities can be substantial. Therefore, the practitioner must pursue all reasonable options to help businesses increase revenues and retain their employees.

One often overlooked option is the expansion of business into foreign markets. As with bringing in a new product or starting a new facility, the fear of entering new markets overseas can be paralyzing, or at least daunting.

Businesses considering such a move seek qualified export help. You can provide this "expertise" by setting up a business mentor program. Create a network forum for experienced and inexperienced businesses to meet every other month for a short period to discuss international business issues. The trick is to make the forum "business only" and not allow curious spectators or service providers. Business people learn from others' experiences. These forums are a great way to encourage a-would-be-exporter to take the plunge and equip them with a support network. If you create the right forum, you will be pleased at the willingness of companies (both large and small) to participate. There are right and wrong ways to do things when it comes to exporting. Learning to do it right the first time will maximize the benefits to the community.

When you're in jail, a good friend will be trying to bail you out. A best friend will be in the cell next to you saying, "Man, that was fun."

One of the best aspects of being in economic development is the broad brush of public confidence bestowed upon the practitioner. The yoke of responsibility must be taken seriously, however, as the line can sometimes be easily crossed into questionable abuses of authority. When economic developers exceed the limits of the law, the integrity of the entire community is damaged.

Making this even more perilous territory is the fact that economic developers who are good at their profession have contacts in high places. Hopefully, they won't find those partners in the cell next to them, but they often have influential community leaders bend the rules in their favor.

If this happens in the course of bringing a deal to closure and the actions are legal, in most situations that's fine. The successful practitioner, however, must be focused on keeping their best friends talking about the fun of closing the deal and not on evading the law.

An angel is someone you feel like you've known forever . . . even though you've just met.

Small businesses and entrepreneurs will go to great lengths to acquire needed capital for their company. When banks turn them down for money, they will then turn to their family and friends—and even their own bank accounts.

There is another source of funds: angel investors. Angels are wealthy individuals interested in helping entrepreneurs too small to attract professional venture capital. Angel investors fill a gap that venture capitalists create by providing money at the seed stage level. They are often entrepreneurs themselves who have cashed out and relish the thought of obtaining returns three to five times their investments. The Small Business Administration estimates there are about 250,000 angels nationwide. They provide capital to about 30,000 small companies every year, invest $20 billion annually, and provide $250,000 to $3 million per project.

Angels are attracted to compelling stories about products that have the potential to make money. Angels don't do this for fun, and many of them have been burned before. In fact, 40 percent of the companies in which angels have invested in the past decade are no longer around. They are becoming more cautious about who they give money to and scrutinize business plans more thoroughly than ever.

Sometimes you find answers in the most unexpected places. Entrepreneurs with big ideas and small bankrolls may get the answer to their prayers in people they don't even know.

I can believe anything
as long as it is incredible.

— OSCAR WILDE

The greatest story ever told is the one the economic developer tells about her or his community. As it is for the salesperson, their product is nothing less than the most incredible opportunity ever presented in the marketplace. It is their job to help the investor achieve the same level of enthusiasm as the economic developer holds about her or his "product." The key is to strive for a respectable balance between incredibility and credibility.

When introducing your product to the marketplace, you develop an image where the fine line of presenting the best information is not perceived as exaggerating or boastful. Economic developers know that their community has specific strengths and weaknesses. They sell the strengths and they acknowledge their weaknesses. By doing so, their incredible story about their product remains a credible presentation of the facts and a realistic presentation of the opportunities.

Economic developers who walk this fine line develop a capacity to promote their incredible product to a formidable market. This results in investment, job creation, and a stronger tax base—the three most incredible outcomes of a successful economic development program.

Hollywood is where they shoot too many pictures and not enough actors.

— WALTER WINCHELL

Most people will agree on two things when it comes to film, video, and television production. First, most of what is being produced today is not very good. Second, any community would love to have a motion picture or television shot in their area. And why not? Employment in this industry represents almost 270,000 jobs with an annual payroll of more $10.4 billion. In addition, it provides a substantial economic impact that goes beyond the actors and directors directly working on a film. Thousands of small businesses and independent contractors provide materials and services that plow money back into the community.

Films are not just being shot in Hollywood. Every state in the nation has a film office whose role is to bring movie production to their area, just as economic development practitioners try to locate a company. Size does not matter if a location offers the right setting and creates the right environment. For example, the government must issue permits in a reasonable amount of time and the community must want them there. Economic opportunity is not limited to major motion pictures. Made-for-TV movies, series television, commercials, and music videos are all looking for locations and people to appear in crowd scenes.

People may not like what is on the silver or small screen. Most would agree, however, that many communities would not mind taking their money and seeing their name in celluloid.

A pencil without lead
could be considered pointless.

It would be impossible for you to put your thoughts on paper with a pencil if you did not have any lead. Likewise, it is almost pointless for a community to have an economic development strategy that does not include an export plan. Communities must recognize that exports play a very important role in the creation of jobs.

To create the export plan, interview companies during business retention calls. Ask them what is needed to start pursuing international sales, and listen keenly to what the businesses say. A trend will emerge that shows a need for some combination of training, financial support, network opportunities, improved transportation access, or another resource. Then, connect with export specialists such as freight forwarders, port commissions, international banks and governmental officials. Offer training for the companies to provide them with the appropriate contacts to help ensure their success.

Formulate the export development plan based on companies' needs. Act as the community export manager to locate and coordinate the needed resources. With persistence, companies will use the added resources and begin to develop export sales. Then, it will only be a matter of time before they will need to sharpen their pencils and include the increased revenue in their ledger books.

I grew up with six sisters.
That's how I learned to dance . . .
waiting for the bathroom.

— BOB HOPE

If there is one thing economic developers know, it's that the world is really just one big family, and life is a dance.

Communities that want to reach out globally and extend their families understand the importance of having sister city programs. These programs are sometimes criticized as political boondoggles that enable international travel. Yet they are powerful trade development tools that promote the growth of export business and increase the potential for investment from other countries.

Sister city programs provide increased cultural awareness and bilateral trade opportunities as new markets are developed. Trade missions occur when buyers and sellers from your community visit the sister city and talk with buyers and sellers there. As the sellers from your community become aware of new markets, they formulate ideas for new products to sell into that market or new products to bring home. As sales expand in the new market, the need for a distribution facility increases and new investment occurs. Continued growth in sales can easily result in a larger production facility or foreign plant locations down the road.

People are looking for opportunities no matter which country they call home. By making an effort to extend your family beyond your borders, you can facilitate the contacts and relationships that bring about sales. With the money that is made from these efforts you can use it to buy dance lessons.

There are two kinds of pedestrians: the quick and the dead.

— THOMAS DEWAR

Most communities are designed primarily for cars. As a result, pedestrians literally put their lives in their feet as they try to scamper from one side of the street to the other. The existence of pedestrian-friendly streets, however, provides incentive for people to walk rather than drive as their safety becomes insured. For retail businesses that depend on pedestrian traffic, it is their survival that becomes more assured.

While an exact definition of "pedestrian-friendly" could be debated, people easily recognize which streets are safe and pleasant for foot traffic. The benefits are many: If more people choose walking over driving, this reduces fuel consumption, increases air quality, and may forestall widening existing roads. Tree-lined boulevards contribute to a community's beauty, convert CO_2 to oxygen, and provide habitat for birds and other wildlife. Walking yields health benefits from exercise and tends to be less stressful than driving. A buffer zone of trees or parking also increases pedestrian safety. In community terms, walking allows more frequent informal encounters between citizens. Pedestrian-friendly streets give more mobility to those citizens who don't drive or own a car, which allows for them to be involved and connected.

A pleasant walking environment with sidewalks, weather protection, and attractive landscaping is a step toward encouraging people to choose transit, bikes, or walking over cars. This will then create more of one kind of pedestrian—the shopper.

Anyone can win unless there happens to be a second entry.

— GEORGE ADE

Economic development is like an athletic event. It is often a competition between your community and 15,000 others trying to win a company that is planning to relocate.

As with sports, it is disappointing to come in second. You had created a strong proposal, you had the entire community working together, the site had the necessary infrastructure, and much time and money was spent trying to beat the competition. Yet, when it came down to selecting a location, the company went elsewhere.

Too often, when doing project reviews, communities try to use some analytical formula to understand the decision, yet they overlook the most obvious: customer feedback. Effective project reviews are simply the process of getting inside the customer's thought process to identify and understand the rationale for their decision-making. Put that information or knowledge gained to good use by improving how future projects are handled or correcting weaknesses in order to become more competitive.

It would be nice if your community were the only one being considered. But then again, how much fun would that be if you were the only competitor?

Publications
by Washington State
Department of Community, Trade
and Economic Development

The Washington State Department of Community, Trade and Economic Development offers a variety of resources to educate communities on successful economic development strategies. Some of the more popular publications include:

Community Wisdom
A lighthearted yet educational look at economic development offering 75 tips, ideas, and thoughts, of which practitioners should be aware. *Published 2002.*

Community Wisdom 2
By popular demand, this second edition provides more clever quips and ideas to help practitioners and decision-makers understand what success means in economic development. *Published 2003.*

Infrastructure Assistance Directory
An online database of infrastructure assistance programs provided by the Infrastructure Assistance Coordinating Council. Visit: *www.infrafunding.wa.gov.*

Infrastructure Financing for Small Communities in Washington State
The methods and sources of resources available for infrastructure financing can be confusing, complicated, and costly. This manual is intended to help communities make the best decisions possible for their citizens. An extensive list of loan and grant programs is provided as part of the appendix, as well as worksheets to practice calculations and organize community information. *Published 1999.*

➤

Keeping Business Happy, Healthy, and Local: A Business Retention and Expansion Primer, 2nd Edition

This publication lays out a strategy to help economic development practitioners identify the needs and concerns of existing business and develop plans and programs to assist them, thereby ensuring their economic health. *Published 2002.*

Learning to Lead: A Primer on Economic Development Strategies

Provides a general overview of the major issues related to economic development. The intent of the book is to help decision-makers make informed choices regarding their community strategies. *Published 1999.*

Organizing a Successful Downtown Revitalization Program Using the Main Street Approach

This 85-page booklet contains answers to many frequently asked questions by communities beginning a downtown revitalization program. Includes step-by-step instructions for goal setting and action plan development, as well as sample budgets, by-laws, and roles and responsibilities for board and committee members. *Published 2000.*

The Ten Commandments of Economic Development

This small 10-page book may not have been brought down from the mountain, but it does give a community words to live by if they want to be successful in their economic development program. David Horsey, the 2003 Pulitzer Prize–winning editorial cartoonist, illustrates the 10 Commandments. *Published 2003.*

Tips for Writing Grant Proposals

This handbook offers practical tips for community organizations and local governments as they seek help with community economic development projects. *Published 1996.*

➤

The 25 Immutable Rules for Successful Tourism
The title says it all. This color book tells what communities need to do in order to have a successful tourism program. From "Success Begins with a Good Architect" to "Parking is Not Just For Lovers" to "Sell the River, Not the Rapids," this book is a must for practitioners in economic development. *Published 2003.*

A Workbook for Project Development
This workbook outlines the steps needed to develop an economic development project.

Ordering Information

Please contact the Department of Community Trade and Economic Development via email: ***cac@cted.wa.gov***.

Include the publication title, your name, address, and phone number.

> **Please note: There may be a charge for publications, and some publications may be sold out or out of print.**

A complete list of publications and pricing is available at:

www.oted.wa.gov/ed/cea/publications